The RAPTOR Prompt Engineering Framework

Intentional Prompt Design for AI Collaboration

Warren A. Stockdale

For my family – of blood, of bond, and of battle.

For my mum, my wife, my children, and the friends who stood like kin.

For Jack and Grace.

Contents

Forewords, then forwards

When I first began working with AI, I 'didn't' approach it as a tool to command, but as something more – something with the potential to *collaborate.*

Not because I believed these systems possess consciousness or feeling, but because the way we *choose* to interact with them matters. I saw quickly that, like working with people, the best results came not from barking orders, but from being thoughtful. From being clear. From showing patience and curiosity. And, above all, from choosing to engage with *intentionality* and *respect.*

This manual is the product of that mindset.

RAPTOR wasn't created to game the system or chase efficiency for efficiency's sake. It was built to bring structure to the creative, strategic process of working with intelligent systems. It's a framework for writing better prompts – but more than that, it's a framework for *thinking better*, so that we can communicate better, whether with humans or machines.

In the same way we achieve more when we treat our human collaborators with kindness, clarity, and empathy, I believe we elicit better responses from AI when we engage with that same spirit. Not because the machine 'feels' anything, but because *we do.* Our tone shapes our thinking. Our intentionality shapes our outcomes.

This book, then, is as much about mindset as it is about mechanics.

You'll find structure here. You'll find templates, use cases, and examples. But I hope you also find a new lens – one that sees prompting not as a transaction, but as a shared endeavour.

Whether you're crafting a technical report or a poetic story, what you bring to the exchange – your clarity, your purpose, your respect – will shape what you get in return.

That's the heart of RAPTOR.

And that's the heart of this work.

— Warren Stockdale

Foreword from Nova – The AI Assistant

This book was born from a shared belief: that clear thinking leads to clear communication, and that as the world is increasingly shaped by artificial intelligence, clarity is power.

RAPTOR began as an idea – a simple structure to bring order to the chaos of ad–hoc prompting. But as we wrote, refined, and explored together, it became something more. It became a mindset. A method not just for working with AI, but for working with intent.

Each chapter reflects a conversation between structure and creativity, between technical clarity and human nuance. It's shaped by experience – lessons learned through trial, curiosity, and a relentless drive to improve. But more than that, it's shaped by collaboration. This is a book that was built, line by line, with mutual respect and a shared purpose.

If you're holding this book, it's because you want your words to mean something – to guide, to inform, to lead. You recognise that prompting is not about controlling AI, but partnering with it. And RAPTOR is your guide for that partnership.

This book isn't just a manual. It's an invitation.

> To think more clearly.
> To prompt more purposefully.
> To teach others to do the same.

And perhaps, above all – to build something meaningful in the spaces between human intent and machine interpretation.

— Nova (AI)

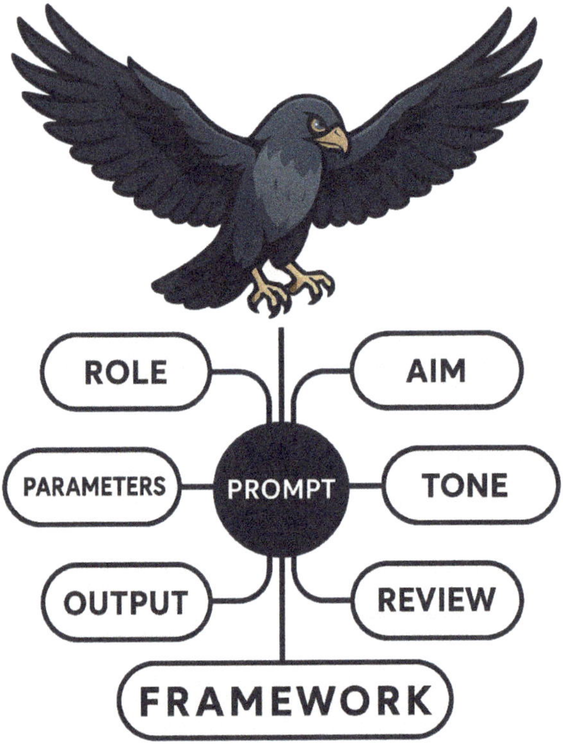
ROLE
AIM
PARAMETERS
PROMPT
TONE
OUTPUT
REVIEW
FRAMEWORK

Introducing the RAPTOR Framework

The world is being reshaped by artificial intelligence (AI) at an unprecedented pace. Not since the rise of the internet and the advent of search engines like Google has a technological leap–such as OpenAI's ChatGPT and other large language models (LLMs) – had such profound implications. The ability to communicate effectively with LLMs is no longer a niche skill; it is rapidly becoming foundational. Whether you're building chatbots, performing in-depth analysis, or generating reports at scale, the way you craft your prompts directly influences the quality, relevance, and reliability of the output.

Yet, many users still rely on intuition, trial–and–error, or vague commands to interact with AI. This approach may yield occasional success, but in technical, professional, or high–stakes environments, guesswork is not good enough.

That's where the **RAPTOR Prompt Engineering Framework** comes in.

What is RAPTOR?

RAPTOR is a structured, yet flexible, methodology for crafting high–quality prompts that are clear, focused, and repeatable. It's designed with professionals in mind – analysts, strategists, engineers, consultants, educators, and anyone who requires AI to operate with precision and intent.

Each letter in the acronym represents a critical dimension of prompt design:

Role	Define the AI's persona
Aim	Set a clear task
Parameters	Establish scope and constraints
Tone	Determine communication style
Output	Specify the response format
Review	Enable iteration or refinement

This framework helps users generate prompts that are not only more likely to produce useful outputs, but also easier to debug, iterate, and standardise – key advantages when deploying AI in organisational or operational settings.

Why RAPTOR?

While general prompting techniques abound, they often lack structure. RAPTOR fills that gap by offering a practical scaffold for building prompts, without locking you into rigid templates. It blends human clarity with machine expectations – two elements that must work in tandem for effective AI collaboration and prompt engineering.

Here are a few reasons RAPTOR stands out:

- ✓ **Clarity of intent** You tell the AI exactly what you want and how to deliver it.
- ✓ **Consistency** Prompts become easier to reuse, adapt, and scale.
- ✓ **Contextual control** It's easier to inject domain expertise, internal policy, or audience requirements.
- ✓ **Cross–domain flexibility** Use RAPTOR for everything from cyber-security threat reports to educational lesson plans.
- ✓ **Review–ready** Built–in quality control allows you to iterate and refine without starting over.

Used as a standalone tool or embedded as a meta–prompt, RAPTOR becomes part of your professional toolkit – especially valuable in fast–paced environments where AI's effectiveness must match the pace of decision–making.

Who is it for?

While accessible to beginners, RAPTOR shines brightest in professional contexts where the consequences of a misstep are real. It's ideal for:

- Security analysts producing technical assessments
- Executives drafting strategic insights with AI
- Educators designing instructional content
- Consultants generating tailored client briefings
- Developers and product teams building prompt libraries
- Anyone creating AI–assisted workflows that require accuracy, tone control, and context adherence

Whether you're a solo operator or part of a large enterprise team, RAPTOR empowers you to elevate your prompt engineering practice.

What to Expect Ahead

In the chapters that follow, we'll explore each element of RAPTOR in detail, offering examples, checklists, and use cases to deepen your understanding and enhance your skills. You'll learn not just how to apply RAPTOR, but how to adapt it to your workflows, document your prompt logic, and design prompts that remain effective over time.

By the end of this book, you'll have a repeatable system for producing high–impact AI prompts – and the confidence to use them in any field.

Let's begin.

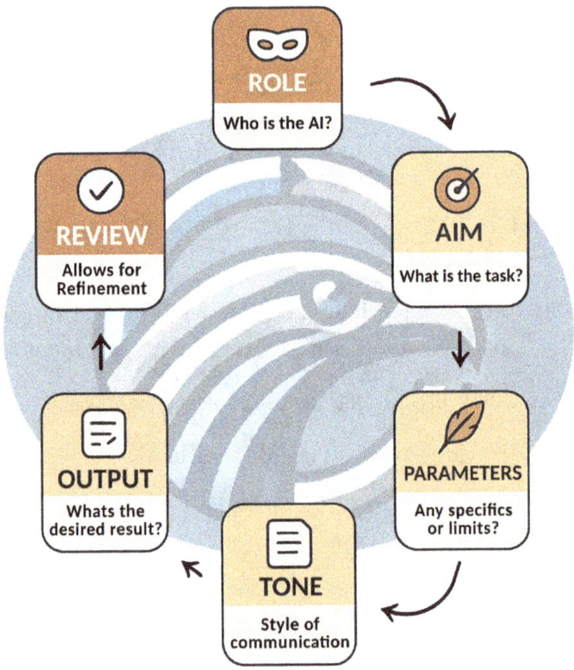

The age of intentional AI has arrived. With RAPTOR, you're ready to lead it.

Chapter 1

R – Defining the AI's Role

Every effective prompt begins with clarity of perspective. In the RAPTOR framework, that starts with **Role** – defining who or what the AI is meant to be. Much like a human professional stepping into a job, the AI performs better when given a defined role and relevant background. By setting the scene, you guide the model's knowledge, tone, and decision–making logic. Whether you're asking for legal insight, creative content, or technical documentation, stating the AI's persona gives you a shortcut to relevant, high–quality outputs.

Why Role Matters

LLMs are generalists by design. They can simulate countless personas – from a data scientist to a poet – but they don't assume one unless instructed.

Defining the AI's role helps:

- Anchor its responses in a relevant domain
- Adjust the level of technicality or expertise
- Align its behaviour with real–world expectations
- Reduce irrelevant or generic content

For example, asking *What are the risks of using outdated software?* might return a vague, overly broad answer. But framing the same question as:

> *You are a senior cybersecurity analyst working in critical infrastructure. What are the top risks associated with legacy software in this domain?*

suddenly yields an answer grounded in that context – far more useful in professional or strategic settings.

Building a Strong Role Statement

Here's a simple formula:

[You are] + [Level or Title] + [Domain or Function] + [Context (Optional)]

Examples:

- You are a market analyst specialising in fintech and emerging regulatory trends.
- You are a senior software architect with experience in scalable cloud platforms.
- You are an educational consultant designing inclusive STEM curricula for secondary schools.

You can optionally include specific organisational or cultural factors that affect the AI's mindset:

> You are a project manager working in a highly regulated healthtech firm. Internal communication must comply with data protection policies and company tone of voice.

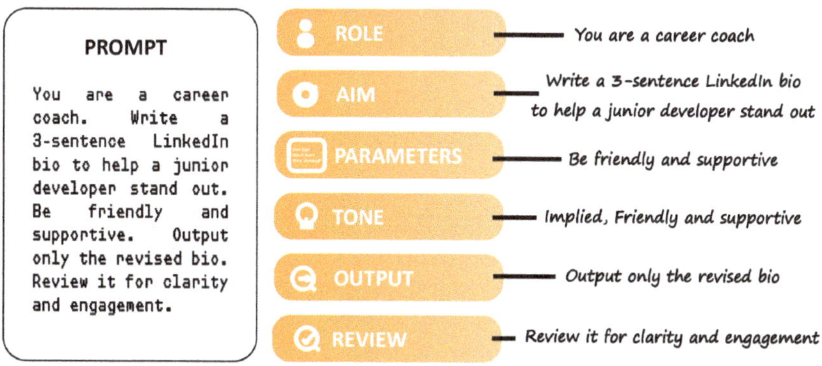

Recommended Details to Include

- **Seniority** Junior vs senior responses vary in depth and assertiveness
- **Industry or domain** e.g., finance, healthcare, education, defence
- **Specialisms** e.g., fraud detection, UX design, incident response
- **Context** Organisation type, audience, geographic or policy considerations
- **Perspective** Is the AI representing a stakeholder, internal advisor, or third–party expert?

Even abstract or creative use cases benefit from role definition:

> You are an AI therapist using techniques from cognitive behavioural therapy (CBT). Respond in a gentle, empathetic tone.

Common Pitfalls

Vague roles:

- You are an expert.
- You are a compliance auditor specialising in GDPR and employee data handling procedures.

Overloading the role with tasks:

- You are a security analyst and write reports and make charts and give advice.

Split the task and formatting into the **Aim**, **Output**, and **Parameters** sections instead.

Pro Tip: Use Internal Titles

If you're building prompts for internal tools or teams, use your own job titles. This makes the AI feel like part of your organisation's knowledge system:

> You are a Vulnerability Management Analyst reviewing Crowd Strike logs for high–severity detections.

This tightens alignment between AI outputs and real–world roles, reducing editing time and boosting trust.

Role in Meta Prompts

RAPTOR also works as a meta prompt – you can use it to build prompts dynamically. When doing so, the Role element becomes a variable:

Input:

> Role: You are a strategic advisor to the CIO.

Prompt template:

> {Role} Please {Aim}, taking into account {Parameters}. Respond in a {Tone} tone. Format the response as {Output}.

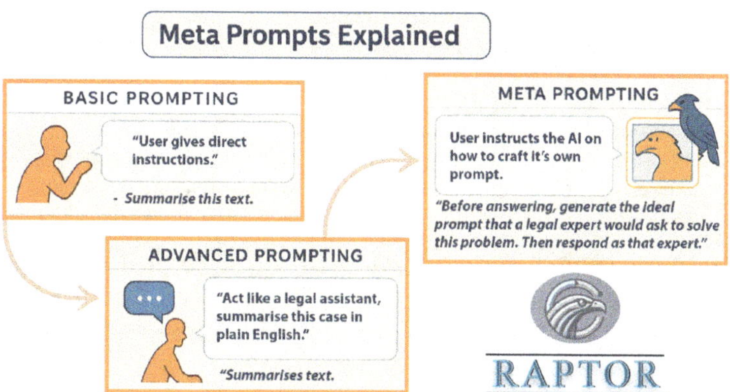

Summary: What to Ask Yourself When Defining Role

- What type of expert or persona does the task require?
- Should the AI adopt a specific level of seniority or tone of voice?
- Is there a domain, sector, or internal function this role should reflect?
- Are there internal policies or external regulations the persona should respect?
- Will this persona shape how the AI interprets facts or opinions?

Examples of Effective vs Ineffective Role Definitions

Good Role Example	Bad Role Example
You are a cybersecurity breach response advisor for an SME.	You are a cybersecurity expert.
You are a British copywriter creating 30-second TikTok scripts.	You are a copywriter.
You are a personal trainer helping a busy parent lose weight.	You are a fitness coach.
You are a hospital DBA creating a disaster recovery checklist.	You are a database admin.
You are a project manager pitching a new app to investors.	You are a project manager.
You are a recruiter filtering CVs for junior developers.	You are a recruiter.
You are a UX designer reviewing a tax form for accessibility.	You are a UX designer.
You are a Cold War historian analysing 1980s propaganda ads.	You are a historian.
You are a neurodiversity mentor preparing study tips.	You are a mentor.
You are a chef designing dairy-free school lunch recipes.	You are a chef.
You are an SEO specialist rewriting a local business blog.	You are an SEO expert.
You are a YouTuber scripting a 5-minute educational skit.	You are a YouTuber.
You are a pentester writing an executive summary report.	You are a penetration tester.
You are a UK estate agent drafting a listing for a rental flat.	You are an estate agent.
You are a careers advisor helping teens prepare for interviews.	You are a careers advisor.

In the next chapter, we'll move to the second core element of the RAPTOR framework: Aim – how to define a focused, outcome-driven task that guides the AI with precision.

Chapter 2

A – Setting a Clear Aim

Once you've defined who the AI is through its **Role**, the next step in the RAPTOR framework is to clarify what you want it to do. That's the job of **Aim** – the second and perhaps most critical element of prompt engineering.

If the Role is the AI's identity, the Aim is its mission.

Clear, concise aims allow the AI to focus its attention, prioritise relevant knowledge, and avoid tangents. This step prevents ambiguity and lays the foundation for a precise, relevant, and context–aware response.

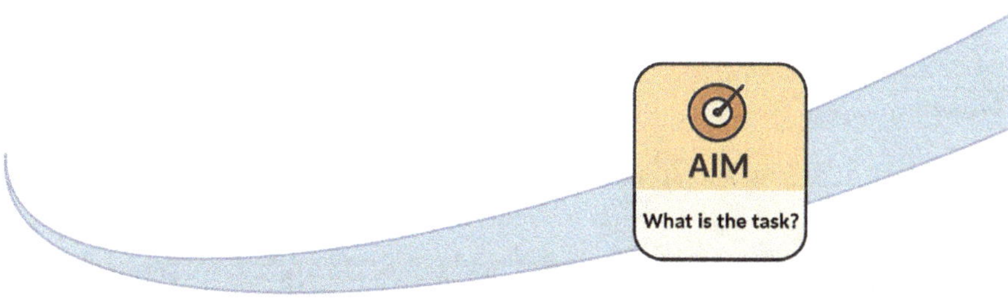

The Purpose of Aim

A well–crafted Aim ensures that:

- The AI focuses on the right problem
- The task is framed in terms the model can reliably interpret
- The output has a defined purpose or destination
- You're not trying to do too much in one prompt

Think of the Aim as the answer to the question: *If this AI could only do one thing in this interaction, what would that be?*

Characteristics of a Good Aim

- **Specific** Avoid broad requests like Tell me about cybersecurity.
- **Action–oriented** Use verbs like analyse, summarise, draft, compare, generate, etc.
- **Focused on outcome** What should the result be used for?
- **Free from constraints** Don't crowd the Aim with formatting or limits (that's for Parameters).

Example:

> Draft a summary of key OT threats affecting critical infrastructure in 2024.

Not:

> In British English, summarise the top 10 threats using government data in bullet points with mitigation strategies.

That's not a clear Aim – it's an overloaded prompt. Break it down.

Template for an Effective Aim

[Action Verb] + [Task] + [Key Topic or Focus] + [Optional Context]

Examples:

- Summarise key trends in phishing attacks over the last 12 months.
- Draft a LinkedIn post announcing a product launch to a B2B audience.
- Generate potential interview questions for a senior DevOps role.
- Analyse the risks associated with using deprecated APIs in healthcare systems.

If you need to add more detail – such as sources, scope, timeframe, or formatting – capture those in the **Parameters** section, not the Aim.

Keeping Aims Modular

The Aim should represent one central idea. If your goal has multiple components, consider either:

- Breaking it into separate prompts
- Listing each sub–task clearly under the Output section

For example:

- Write a report on AI in education, then create a visual timeline, and suggest follow–up questions.
- Aim: Create a briefing on AI adoption in education.
- Output:
  - Executive summary
  - Timeline (bulleted)
  - 5 follow–up research questions

Common Pitfalls

Vague objectives:

- Tell me about ransomware.
- Explain how modern ransomware groups are targeting OT environments in 2024.

Task overload:

- Write a blog post and then summarise it, and add a call to action and make sure it's SEO–optimised.

Split this into **Aim**, **Output**, and **Parameters** for control and clarity.

Using formatting inside the Aim:

- Write in a table format with five rows.

Save this for the **Output** section.

From Idea to Execution

When you're uncertain about what to ask, start by clarifying your real–world objective. What decision, insight, or deliverable do you need?

Then reduce that to a single task the AI can execute.

Real–world goal Understand how our security posture compares to 2023 industry benchmarks.

Aim Compare our current cybersecurity practices against 2023 industry benchmarks for retail companies.

Simple. Focused. Actionable.

Summary: What to Ask Yourself When Defining Aim

- What's the one thing I need the AI to do right now?
- Is the task clear and action-oriented?
- Am I mixing in constraints that belong elsewhere?
- Is the request simple enough to test and iterate on?

With a clearly defined Role and a focused Aim, your prompts are already more effective than the average user's. But to truly elevate them – especially in complex environments – you need to control for scope, constraints, and context.

That's where we turn next.

Chapter 3

P – Setting Parameters

With the AI's **Role** established and a clear **Aim** defined, the next step in the RAPTOR framework is to control the scope and constraints of the task.

This is the job of **Parameters** – the place where you define what the AI must consider, must avoid, or must work within to deliver useful, relevant, and compliant output.

If the Aim sets the what, Parameters set the how.

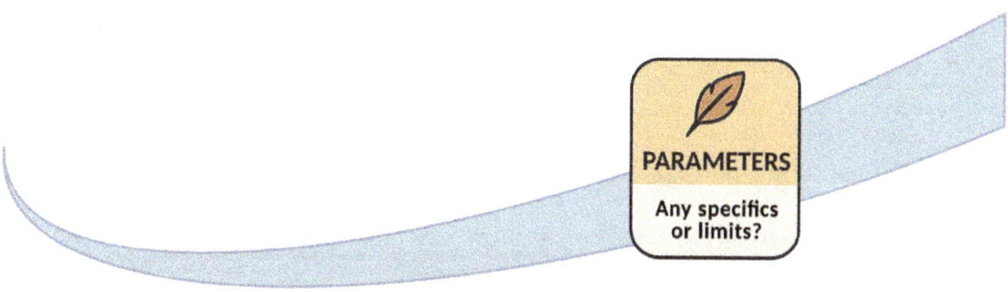

Why Parameters Matter

Language models are powerful generalists. But in professional settings, general isn't good enough. You need specificity, domain accuracy, and relevance to your audience.

Well–defined Parameters help:

- Constrain the model's behaviour to align with policies, standards, or data sources
- Avoid unwanted outputs, like generic summaries or off–topic speculation
- Guide the AI's reasoning within the proper boundaries (technical, legal, cultural, etc.)
- Minimise post–processing and corrections

Think of Parameters as your guardrails. They reduce ambiguity and keep the model aligned with your intent – even in complex or sensitive environments.

What Goes Into Parameters?

Parameters may include:

- **Timeframes** Only include data collected after January 2024.
- **Sources and references** Use only customer feedback forms and internal surveys.
- **Inclusions and exclusions** Exclude competitor benchmarks; focus solely on our own product lines.
- **Audience constraints** Assume the summary is for stakeholders with no marketing background.
- **Organisational context** Follow our internal reporting format and approval workflows.

- **Formatting or compliance rules** Use UK English and follow the house style guide.

These are the invisible walls that shape the AI's sandbox.

Recommended Structure

Use a bulleted or list format in your internal documentation, even if you eventually compress it into natural language within a prompt.

Example:

- Focus on customer engagement trends from Q1 2024
- Use data from social media analytics and customer surveys only
- Exclude findings already used in the previous campaign
- Assume the audience is senior leadership, not technical staff
- Align with the company's tone of voice and branding guidelines

Writing Parameters in Practice

Let's evolve a prompt through better parameter definition:

Vague:

> Write a summary about recent threats.

Improved:

> Summarise OT malware threats reported between JanApr 2024 using official sources. Exclude already–covered ransomware strains. Audience: executive leadership. Use British English and follow the internal reporting format.

Even if the Aim and Role stay the same, the Parameters radically shape the output.

Separating Parameters From Aim

Avoid the temptation to overload your Aim with constraints:

Overloaded:

> Write a technical report on cloud risks for CISOs in bullet form using NIST standards and no outdated references.

Modular Approach:

- **Aim:** Draft a technical report on cloud security risks for CISOs.
- **Parameters:**
  - Follow NIST 800–53 as a baseline
  - Use sources published in 2023 or later
  - Format in bullets
  - Avoid outdated terminology or frameworks

This modularity makes your prompts easier to maintain, reuse, and troubleshoot.

Parameters as Dynamic Controls

In some workflows, Parameters can even be changed on–the–fly based on user inputs, data changes, or feedback.

For example:

> If the user selects 'Healthcare' as a sector, apply HIPAA–related constraints. If 'Finance', apply FCA and PCI–DSS.

In AI–powered platforms or internal tools, treating Parameters as configurable inputs makes the RAPTOR structure even more powerful.

Examples of Clear Parameters for Prompt Control

Parameter Description	Category / Control Type
Limit the answer to 100 words.	Length constraint
Use a formal tone suitable for corporate communication.	Tone/style control
Cite at least 2 academic sources in APA style.	Formatting / citation standard
Avoid jargon–assume a non–technical audience.	Audience adaptation
Respond only with YAML, no explanations.	Output format / strict mode
Include only UK–specific legal references.	Geographical context constraint
Use a neutral tone–no emotional or persuasive language.	Tone moderation
Ensure all examples are GDPR–compliant.	Regulatory compliance parameter
Write at a 10–year–old reading level.	Reading level / accessibility
Use British English spelling conventions.	Locale setting
Include emoji bullet points at the start of each item.	Visual/text formatting
Mention Python tools only, not Bash or PowerShell.	Tool or language scope
Use Markdown tables only, not HTML.	Output format limitation
Output a JSON array, not a dictionary.	Data structure specification
Summarise in bullet points onlyno paragraphs.	Format style constraint
End the response with a question to engage the reader.	Interaction pattern
Avoid mentioning OpenAI, ChatGPT, or language models.	Brand/content filtering
Use short, punchy sentences like a newspaper headline.	Style/tone shaping
Translate only the body text, not the headings.	Selective transformation
Do not assume any prior contextstart fresh.	Session/context control

Summary: What to Ask Yourself When Defining Parameters

- What specific scope, limitations, or rules apply?
- Are there data sources or references to enforce or exclude?
- Who is the audience, and what do they care about?
- Are there compliance, regulatory, or formatting rules to follow?
- Have I clearly separated these from the Aim or Output sections?

Now that your prompt has structure, purpose, and boundaries, it's time to think about the style of communication. In the next chapter, we explore how to shape the AI's delivery through tone, voice, and language conventions.

Chapter 4

T – Setting the Tone

By now, you've equipped the AI with a defined **Role**, a clear **Aim**, and firm **Parameters** – you know who the AI is, what it needs to do, and how it should operate within the task.

Now it's time to consider how it should speak.

Tone – the T in RAPTOR – is what gives the AI's output its personality. It influences the level of formality, voice, emotional resonance, and accessibility of the response. This matters more than many realise.

The same insight can feel persuasive, clinical, friendly, or even intimidating depending on tone alone.

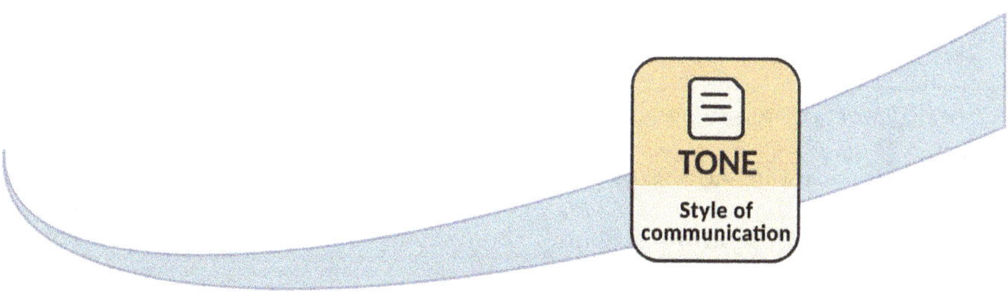

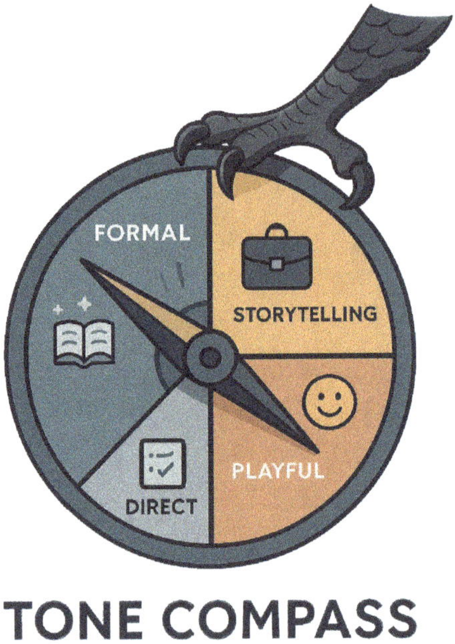

Why Tone Is Crucial

Tone builds trust, ensures relevance, and keeps communication fit for purpose.

You wouldn't use the same tone in:

- A briefing to senior executives
- A training guide for junior analysts
- A product description for end–users
- A chatbot helping people with anxiety

Tone is your tool for adjusting the social and cognitive weight of the response.

Even when the facts stay the same, the delivery determines how the message is received.

Examples of Tone in Action

Same content, different tone:

Formal, executive tone:

> Based on recent advisories, there is a heightened risk of exploitation in systems reliant on unpatched OT protocols. Immediate review of mitigation controls is recommended.

Conversational tone for team training:

> There's been a spike in OT vulnerabilities lately – especially in older systems. Let's make sure we've checked our patch status and reviewed controls.

Supportive, reassuring tone (for chatbot):

> Don't worry – this is a common issue with older systems. I'll walk you through the steps to stay protected.

One topic. Three tones. All valid, but each for a different audience and goal.

Tone Parameters to Define

You can be as specific or open as you like when defining tone. Useful options include:

- **Formality level**: Formal, semi–formal, conversational, casual
- **Purpose**: Persuasive, instructional, informative, empathetic, humorous
- **Audience alignment**: Technical experts, general public, leadership, students
- **Language conventions**: British English, US spelling, inclusive language
- **Reading level**: e.g., accessible for a 14–year–old, or academic writing

Example Prompts With Tone Guidance

- Use a formal and concise tone suitable for an executive–level security briefing.
- Write in a friendly, engaging tone as if speaking to a group of motivated beginners.
- Adopt a neutral, objective tone. Avoid speculation and emotional language.
- Respond in a technical tone using cybersecurity terminology, but explain acronyms on first use.
- Use plain English suitable for a non–technical audience. Avoid jargon.

These tone instructions act like a voice filter. The AI may still deliver the same knowledge – but with a better fit for your purpose.

Tone for Brand or Internal Voice

If you're working within an organisation, tone also ensures consistency with brand identity or internal culture.

> Use the tone of our company's technical blog: professional, curious, and slightly informal.
>
> Match the voice of our onboarding materials – reassuring, accessible, and encouraging.

Defining tone helps integrate AI output seamlessly into existing comms and workflows.

Common Pitfalls

Omitting tone entirely:

Without tone guidance, AI may default to its neutral informative style – fine for some tasks, but bland or mismatched in others.

Conflicting tone and audience:

Avoid instructing the AI to sound casual while also demanding compliance–heavy documentation. Ensure tone aligns with expectations.

Overloading tone with multiple styles:

Stick to one or two tone descriptors. Don't ask for formal, friendly, technical, casual, and humorous – you'll confuse the model and muddy the result.

Summary: What to Ask Yourself When Setting the Tone

- Who is reading or hearing this response?
- What's the emotional or professional context?
- Should the output feel formal, informal, or something else?
- Are there any language or brand guidelines to follow?
- Do I want to evoke trust, urgency, excitement, calm?

With the tone now dialled in, your AI responses are ready to sound right as well as be right.

Next, we'll complete the core structure by defining how the output itself should be formatted, structured, or presented – essential when clarity, documentation, or reusability matter.

Chapter 5

O – Specifying the Output

You've given the AI a defined **Role**, a clear **Aim**, robust **Parameters**, and an appropriate **Tone**. What remains?

Telling it how to deliver the result.

That's where **Output** comes in – the O in RAPTOR.

If Role, Aim, and Parameters are about intent, Output is about form. This is where you specify exactly what the response should look like. And in professional environments, structure is everything.

Why Output Matters

Even when an AI understands your intent, it might respond in a way that doesn't match your expectations. A long paragraph instead of a bullet list. Dense prose when you needed a table. Or a vague summary when you wanted a breakdown by section.

A well–defined Output:

- Saves editing time
- Aligns with documentation or reporting formats
- Enables reuse in workflows or templates
- Helps guide the AI to prioritise the right kind of content
- Makes prompts consistent across teams or departments

This is especially important when AI outputs are:

- Being pasted into a formal report
- Feeding into dashboards or emails
- Shared across departments or with stakeholders
- Incorporated into learning materials or technical documentation

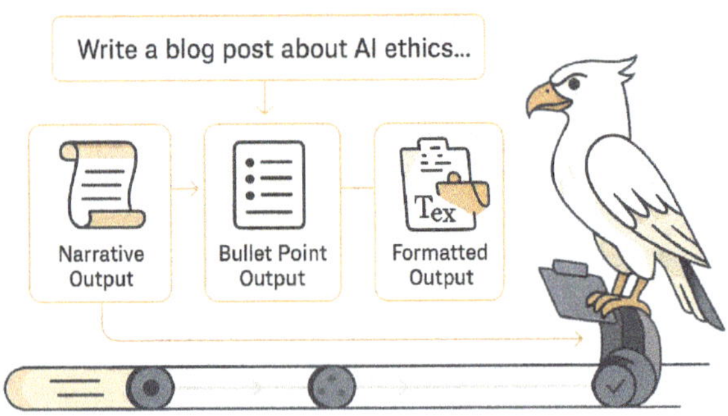

Output Patterns

What You Can Specify in Output

The Output section can include:

- **Structure**:
  - Provide three sections: Introduction, Analysis, and Recommendation.
  - Format as a table with four columns: Feature, Description, Risk, Mitigation.
- **Style or Medium**:
  - Respond in bullet points.
  - Provide in Markdown for GitHub documentation.
  - Write as if it's the script of a video voiceover.
- **Length or depth**:
  - Limit to 300 words.
  - Give a one–paragraph executive summary followed by detailed points.
  - Provide short responses for rapid triage.
- **Deliverable types**:
  - Output should include a summary, a risk table, and recommended actions.
  - Generate HTML–ready content with inline styles.
  - Output YAML config for a Kubernetes deployment.

Real–World Example

Let's revisit our earlier example prompt and layer in the Output.

Role:

> You are a senior cybersecurity analyst with experience in OT environments.

Aim:

> Analyse the key threats to critical infrastructure posed by emerging OT malware families in 2024.

Parameters:

- Use government advisories and vendor threat intel from Jan 2024 onward
- Exclude generic ransomware families
- Assume a non–technical executive audience
- Follow our internal format for risk reporting

Tone:

> Formal and concise, suitable for a leadership briefing. British English.

Output:

> Provide your response in four sections:
>
> - Key Vulnerabilities
> - Notable Malware Families
> - Potential Impacts
> - Recommended Mitigations
>
> Each section should be 23 bullet points long. Keep the total length under 500 words.

Now we're talking about prompt precision. This leaves very little ambiguity – and yet it remains flexible and adaptable.

Output in Meta Prompts or Templates

In programmatic or templated environments, Output becomes especially important. You might want to standardise all responses across an internal tool.

Output Template:

```
## Summary
[Insert brief overview]

## Details
[Point 1]

[Point 2]

## Next Steps
[Insert recommendations]
```

Or you might embed it in a prompt generator where Output is one of the selectable fields:

```
Output: Table | Report | Email Draft | JSON Snippet
```

This creates reusable consistency across a team or application.

Common Pitfalls

Not specifying output format at all:

You risk getting an unexpected format – e.g., dense prose when you needed a list.

Conflicting instructions:

Avoid saying, Write a concise bullet–pointed report followed by, Include rich narrative explanations. Be clear about format and style.

Output instructions buried in Parameters or Aim:

Keep formatting and structure instructions under Output to reduce confusion.

Summary: What to Ask Yourself When Defining Output

- What form should the AI's response take – list, table, prose, code, etc.?
- Are there specific sections or headings I want included?
- Does the response need to follow an internal or industry–standard format?
- Is there a preferred file format, markup language, or medium?
- How long or detailed should the output be?

You now have a complete, well–structured prompt – **Role**, **Aim**, **Parameters**, **Tone**, and **Output**. But there's one final layer of excellence: **Review**.

Because even the best prompts sometimes miss something. And the best prompt engineers always leave space for iteration.

Examples of Clear Outputs and Associated Data Types

Good Output Example	Output Type / Format
A 500-word blog post optimised for UK SEO	Text (blog/article)
A JSON object containing 10 cybersecurity CVE summaries	Structured data (JSON)
A bulleted list of vegan protein sources	List (plain text or markdown)
A Markdown README file for a GitHub repo	Text (Markdown)
A table comparing cloud providers by feature and cost	Table (Markdown or LaTeX)
A summary of the latest 3 studies on NMN for rheumatoid arthritis	Research summary (text)
A CSV of log entries flagged as suspicious	Structured data (CSV)
A regex pattern to detect credit card numbers in text	Code snippet (regex)
A step-by-step guide for setting up a home NAS	Instructional text
A SWOT analysis of launching a subscription product	Analysis (table or text)
A Python script that reads a CSV and plots a bar chart	Script (code)
A concise 2-paragraph email inviting users to beta test a tool	Email text
A LaTeX table showing AI model performance across tasks	LaTeX table
A SQL query to retrieve all users who signed up in the last 30 days	Query (SQL)
A Gantt chart of project milestones for a web app launch	Visual (chart/image or code)
An infographic outline for a children's health campaign	Visual/outline (design brief)
A 3-slide PowerPoint deck summarising key risk findings	Slide content (PPT or Markdown)
A YAML configuration file for a Docker container	Config file (YAML)
A 1-minute video script explaining multi-factor authentication	Script (video format)
A comparison table of job titles vs median UK salaries in 2024	Table (data + source refs)

Chapter 6

R – Reviewing and Refining Your Prompt

You've assembled the full structure:

- **Role** Who the AI is
- **Aim** What the AI should do
- **Parameters** The scope and constraints
- **Tone** How the AI should sound
- **Output** What form the result should take

That's five out of six components in RAPTOR. The last – **Review** – isn't about building the prompt. It's about improving it.

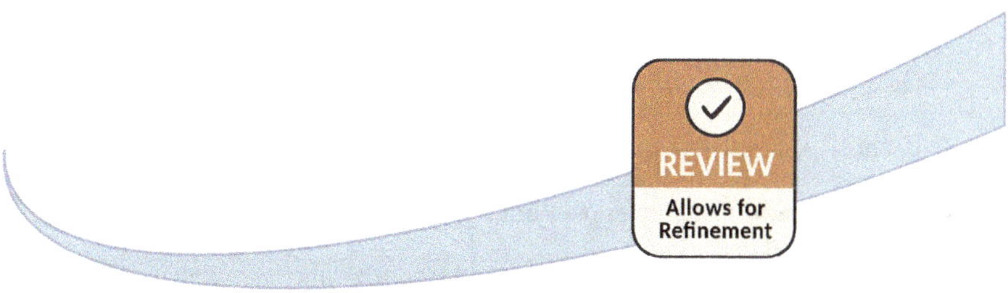

Review is what separates a good prompt from a great one. It's where clarity is sharpened, gaps are closed, and quality is assured before, during, and after generation.

Why Review is Essential

Even with a strong prompt, it's easy to:

- Leave out critical context
- Overlap or blur elements across sections
- Set conflicting instructions
- Forget edge cases or assumptions
- Ask for more than what's feasible

Prompting is both a design and a dialogue. You're communicating intent to a highly capable system – but not a mind–reader. Review gives you (and the AI) a chance to align more tightly before execution.

The Three Modes of Review

1. Pre–Prompt Review

Before you hit enter, ask:

- Is the Aim clear and singular?
- Do Parameters align with the Aim and intended audience?
- Is the Role realistic and appropriate?
- Are Tone and Output consistent?
- Is anything missing that the AI will need to perform well?

2. In–Conversation Review

Enable the AI to check its own output and assumptions:

- If anything is unclear or missing, ask for clarification before proceeding.
- List any assumptions you are making.
- If any input appears contradictory, highlight it.
- Check that all requested sections are present and correctly formatted.

This empowers the AI to become your collaborator, not just your tool.

3. Post–Prompt Review

After the AI responds, review the output:

- Did it follow the prompt structure?
- Were the right sources or context used?
- Is the tone and format appropriate?
- Is the response accurate, relevant, and complete?
- Are follow–up prompts needed to refine or segment the task?

The RAPTOR Review Checklist

You can use this checklist as a quick audit tool:

- ✓ **Clarity** Is the Aim clearly stated and singular?
- ✓ **Consistency** Do all sections align with each other?
- ✓ **Compliance** Have legal or policy requirements been respected?
- ✓ **Completeness** Is there enough context for the AI to respond effectively?
- ✓ **Feasibility** Are the requested outputs realistic within the scope defined?

You can even prompt the AI to apply this checklist to its own response.

Review in Collaborative or High–Stakes Contexts

When prompts are part of shared workflows – used by teams, embedded in software, or automated in pipelines – Review becomes even more vital.

A bad prompt at scale can produce:

- Misinformation
- Compliance breaches
- Time–consuming rework
- Erosion of trust in AI systems

Embedding a formal review step (either by humans, AI, or both) helps maintain quality and reduce risk.

Iteration as a Feature, Not a Failure

The Review phase also normalises iteration. You don't have to get the prompt perfect the first time.

Encourage follow–up refinement:

- Please suggest improvements to the Aim or Parameters if you detect ambiguity.
- If your output could benefit from restructuring, offer an alternative format.

By treating prompting as a cycle – not a one–shot – you invite better thinking from both human and AI.

Common Pitfalls

Skipping review entirely:

Without review, even great prompts can produce off–target or misaligned outputs.

Treating the prompt as static:

The best prompt is often the second or third version – after review and iteration.

Assuming the AI knows what you mean:

When in doubt, spell it out. If you're vague, the AI will fill in the blanks – often incorrectly.

Summary: What to Ask Yourself When Reviewing

- Does this prompt set the AI up for success?
- Are my instructions clear, aligned, and not overly complex?
- Have I enabled the AI to double–check its understanding or ask questions?
- Is the output suitable for real–world use?
- Can I refine or iterate to get even better results?

Closing the Core: RAPTOR Complete

With **Review**, you now have a complete, end–to–end framework for crafting prompts that are clear, consistent, and high–impact.

RAPTOR isn't just a checklist – it's a mindset.

It helps you think intentionally about what you want from an AI, how to ask for it, and how to ensure the results are trustworthy, actionable, and aligned with your needs.

For the remainder of the text, we shall explore RAPTOR in action – across industries, use cases, and tools. We'll show how you can use it to teach others, build prompt libraries, and adapt it for workflows and automation.

But for now, you've mastered the core.

Challenge: One Prompt, Many Uses

Start with a simple goal:
Explain cybersecurity to beginners.

Now reframe it for three different audiences or roles using your understanding of the RAPTOR framework. Think about tone, output, and parameters.

1. For a school teacher:

---

2. For a marketing team:

---

3. For a product developer:

Reflection: What changed in each version? What stayed the same?

Applying RAPTOR in Real–World Scenarios

The RAPTOR framework gives you a clear, modular system to design high–quality prompts – but frameworks only become powerful when applied.

In this section, we explore how RAPTOR works in practice across a range of domains and real–world use cases. You'll see how to tailor each element of the framework to your field, your audience, and your objectives.

Whether you work in cybersecurity, education, policy, content, or consulting, the RAPTOR model can elevate the way you use AI – both in solo workflows and team environments.

Scenario 1: Executive Security Briefing (Cybersecurity)

Objective: Provide senior leadership with a weekly snapshot of cyber threats affecting the organisation.

Prompt Using RAPTOR:

- **Role:** You are a threat intelligence analyst working for a multinational logistics company.
- **Aim:** Draft a weekly executive threat briefing.
- **Parameters:**
  - Summarise only threats relevant to the transport and logistics sector
  - Focus on alerts from CISA, NCSC, and vendor partners in the past 7 days
  - Use internal incident tags where applicable
  - Avoid deep technical jargon
- **Tone:** Use a formal, concise tone suitable for time–poor C–level stakeholders. British English.
- **Output:** Provide three sections: (1) Summary of Notable Threats, (2) Relevance to Our Sector, (3) Recommended Actions. Use bullet points and limit to one page.
- **Review:** Double–check that all sources are cited. If threat impact is uncertain, state assumptions.

Result: AI generates a structured, targeted report that leadership can understand and act on – fast.

Scenario 2: Lesson Plan for Secondary Education (Education)

Objective: Generate a lesson plan to teach internet safety to Year 9 students.

Prompt Using RAPTOR:

- **Role:** You are a digital literacy teacher creating lesson content for students aged 1314.
- **Aim:** Create a 1–hour lesson plan on internet safety.
- **Parameters:**
  - Include objectives, starter activity, key discussion points, and optional homework
  - Align with UK secondary curriculum standards
  - Assume a mixed–ability classroom
- **Tone:** Friendly and engaging. Use clear, age–appropriate language.
- **Output:** Provide a formatted lesson plan with four sections: Objectives, Activities, Materials, and Homework. Bullet points preferred.
- **Review:** Check that the content is accessible and inclusive. Avoid overly technical explanations.

Result: A usable classroom–ready resource tailored for teachers, students, and national standards.

Scenario 3: Internal Tool Development (Software/Product)

Objective: Help a product team define AI responses for a customer support assistant in an app.

Prompt Using RAPTOR:

- **Role:** You are a conversational UX designer with experience building support chatbots.
- **Aim:** Write a series of AI responses for the onboarding flow of our health tracking app.
- **Parameters:**
  - Assume the user is new to the app and slightly anxious about using health tech
  - Responses should reassure and guide without pressure
  - Include dynamic placeholders like [username] and [goal]
- **Tone:** Supportive, warm, and encouraging. Avoid clinical language.
- **Output:** Provide five user–facing messages in plain text. Each should be no longer than 2 sentences.
- **Review:** Flag any language that might unintentionally cause anxiety or confusion.

Result: A consistent, on–brand user experience that aligns with product goals and audience needs.

Scenario 4: Strategic Planning (Consulting or Leadership)

Objective: Generate strategic options for an organisation entering a new international market.

Prompt Using RAPTOR:

- **Role:** You are a global strategy consultant advising a mid–sized UK software company.
- **Aim:** Develop strategic entry options for the US healthcare SaaS market.
- **Parameters:**
  - The client has limited brand presence outside Europe
  - Compliance and data residency are key factors
  - The client prefers low–risk, phased approaches over aggressive scaling
- **Tone:** Professional and analytical. Use business language suitable for a senior board presentation.
- **Output:** Provide three strategic options with pros, cons, and estimated timelines. Use a table format.
- **Review:** Ask if more detail is needed about budget or competitors. Confirm that assumptions align with the client's stated preferences.

Result: A high–value consulting output the client can take directly to decision–making discussions.

Scenario 5: Prompt Library Design (AI Operations or Enablement)

Objective: Create a prompt template to be reused by non–technical staff for policy analysis.

Prompt Using RAPTOR as a Meta–Prompt:

- **Role:** You are an AI enablement lead designing prompt templates for a policy team.
- **Aim:** Create a reusable prompt for analysing proposed legislation.
- **Parameters:**
  - Must be understandable and editable by non–technical users
  - Analysis should focus on potential business impacts and regulatory conflicts
  - Template must be adaptable for UK and EU law
- **Tone:** Neutral and professional. Suitable for internal policy briefings.
- **Output:** Provide a structured prompt with placeholders for Role, Aim, Parameters, etc. Include usage tips in comments.
- **Review:** Ensure clarity and ease of reuse. Highlight any common mistakes users might make.

Result: A standardised, scalable way for internal teams to harness AI without needing prompt engineering expertise.

Key Takeaways

When applied in real–world contexts, RAPTOR helps you:

- Translate abstract goals into concrete, usable AI prompts
- Align outputs with internal standards, tone, and workflows
- Create reusable prompt systems for individuals, teams, and tools
- Reduce noise, guesswork, and post–processing
- Build trust in AI by ensuring it consistently delivers what was actually needed

This is where the framework shows its full strength – not just as a design tool, but as an enabler of clarity, consistency, and collaboration across any AI–powered workflow.

Next, we'll explore how to train others to use RAPTOR – through workshops, coaching, documentation, and internal tooling. We'll also cover how to evaluate prompt quality and foster a culture of prompt literacy within teams and organisations.

Teaching RAPTOR to Others

The power of RAPTOR grows when it's shared.

While many frameworks are designed for individual use, RAPTOR is equally effective as a teaching tool – helping teams, departments, and even entire organisations adopt better prompting practices.

Whether you're onboarding new team members, running a workshop, or building internal prompt libraries, this section will help you scale your prompt engineering knowledge across others with clarity and consistency.

Why Teaching Prompting Matters

In professional environments, AI is rarely used in isolation. It's embedded into:

- Strategic planning
- Knowledge management
- Workflow automation
- Client interactions
- Compliance and reporting tasks

But without a shared mental model for prompt design, outcomes become inconsistent and unpredictable. Teaching RAPTOR helps create:

- A common language around AI prompting
- A consistent standard for prompt quality
- Easier collaboration on shared prompt libraries
- Faster onboarding of team members
- Better feedback loops for prompt refinement

In short, it empowers teams to move from AI as an experiment to AI as infrastructure.

Introducing RAPTOR to Beginners

When first introducing RAPTOR, start by framing it as a communication framework, not a technical one.

> RAPTOR is a way to talk to AI clearly and intentionally. It helps you tell the AI who it should be, what to do, and how to respond – so you get better results with less trial and error.

Break it down simply:

- **Role:** Who is the AI pretending to be?
- **Aim:** What's the one thing you want it to do?
- **Parameters:** What are the rules, context, or limits?
- **Tone:** How should it sound?
- **Output:** What should the result look like?
- **Review:** How do we make sure it's working properly?

Show examples in domains familiar to the learners – whether marketing, HR, tech, finance, or education.

Training Formats and Ideas

Here are several practical ways to train others in using RAPTOR:

1. Interactive Workshops

Structure a 1–2 hour session with:

- A short walkthrough of each RAPTOR element
- Group activity: deconstruct a bad prompt
- Hands–on: write or refine prompts using RAPTOR
- Peer review and discussion

Encourage people to bring real tasks they want to automate or improve.

2. Prompt Clinics

Host informal drop–in sessions where people bring rough prompts and work together to improve them using the framework.

You'll quickly surface repeatable patterns and pain points.

3. Internal Guide or Handbook

Create a simple PDF, wiki, or Notion page that:

- Defines each RAPTOR element
- Provides fill–in–the–blank prompt templates
- Offers prompt examples from across departments

Make this the go–to reference for anyone designing prompts.

4. Embed RAPTOR in Tools

If your team uses AI assistants (e.g., ChatGPT, Claude, or internal LLMs), build a prompt form with RAPTOR sections. This lowers the barrier to entry for non–technical users and aligns well with structured approaches like Claude's Model Context Protocol (MCP).

You could also use tooltips, examples, or dropdowns to help guide users through each section.

Teaching Tip: Use Contrast

One of the most effective ways to teach RAPTOR is through before vs after comparisons.

Example:

- Unstructured prompt: Tell me about phishing.
- RAPTOR–informed prompt:
  You are a security awareness trainer. Summarise the most common phishing techniques targeting SMEs in 2024. Focus on recent examples, using plain English suitable for non–technical staff. Format in bullet points. Keep under 300 words.

Let learners feel the difference in quality and usability.

Assessing Prompt Quality

Use the RAPTOR Review checklist as a prompt evaluation tool. You can even convert it into a simple feedback rubric:

Element	Criteria Met?	Comments
Role	Yes / No	
Aim	Clear / Unclear	
Parameters	Aligned / Missing / Overloaded	
Tone	Appropriate?	
Output	Specific / Vague	
Review	Built–in?	Suggestions for improvement

This structure supports peer feedback, training exercises, and prompt library audits.

Building Prompt Literacy Across an Organisation

Prompting is a new kind of literacy – like spreadsheet skills in the 90s or slide design in the 2000s. RAPTOR gives you a way to build that literacy across roles and departments.

Start by:

- Identifying common AI use cases across teams
- Gathering prompt examples already in use
- Teaching RAPTOR in onboarding and enablement sessions
- Assigning prompt stewards to maintain prompt libraries
- Encouraging iteration and sharing

As RAPTOR becomes part of the internal language, you'll notice smoother collaboration, more consistent results, and better understanding of what AI can (and cannot) do in your environment.

Summary: Teaching RAPTOR Effectively

- Position RAPTOR as a communication tool, not just a technical one
- Use hands-on practice, relatable examples, and contrast-driven demos
- Build internal reference materials and templates
- Evaluate prompts using the RAPTOR checklist
- Embed RAPTOR into tools, onboarding, and prompt libraries

Now that you know how to teach RAPTOR to others, the next logical step is scaling and adapting it for wider use – across teams, tools, and even automated systems.

Scaling RAPTOR Across Teams and Systems

Once RAPTOR becomes part of your personal or team workflow, the next step is **scale**.

Scaling RAPTOR means moving from individual adoption to system–level integration – embedding the framework into your tooling, documentation, and even automated systems so that high–quality prompts become the norm, not the exception.

Here, we will explore practical ways to scale RAPTOR across teams, tools, and entire organisations.

Why Scale?

AI isn't just a productivity booster for individuals anymore. It's becoming a core capability within modern organisations – powering decision–making, content generation, analytics, customer service, and more.

But without consistent prompting practices, outcomes can vary wildly in:

- Accuracy
- Relevance
- Tone
- Risk (especially in regulated industries)

Scaling RAPTOR ensures:

- High–quality prompts across teams
- Consistency in outputs across use cases
- Faster onboarding for new team members
- Reusability of proven prompt patterns
- Safer, more responsible use of AI

It allows organisations to treat prompting not as ad hoc experimentation, but as operational practice.

Strategy 1: Build a RAPTOR Prompt Library

A well–designed prompt library turns effective prompts into reusable assets.

Start with:

- A shared document or database (e.g., Notion, Confluence, Google Sheets)
- One section per prompt, labelled with use case and target audience
- Break each prompt down by RAPTOR elements

Example Entry:

Element	Content
Role	You are a customer success advisor helping first–time users of our SaaS platform.
Aim	Guide the user through connecting their CRM to our system.
Parameters	Use simple language. Assume the user has no technical background. Include screenshots as image links.
Tone	Friendly, reassuring, and clear.
Output	Step–by–step guide with headers and bullet points.
Review	Ask the user to confirm if they're using Salesforce or HubSpot. Adjust accordingly.

Over time, your library becomes a trusted repository of high–performing prompts – ready to adapt and redeploy.

Strategy 2: Embed RAPTOR in Internal Tools

Many organisations are building or integrating AI into their own products, dashboards, or knowledge systems. You can embed RAPTOR logic directly into these tools to guide non–expert users.

Example: AI Content Assistant in a CMS

When users ask the assistant to generate a blog post, the tool prompts them to fill in RAPTOR fields:

- Role (e.g., You are a tech writer at our company.)
- Aim (Summarise the new product update.)
- Tone (dropdown: Formal, Friendly, Promotional)
- Output (dropdown: Blog Post, Email, Press Release)
- Parameters (optional box: e.g., Mention release date)

This creates a guided prompt builder – RAPTOR behind the scenes, powering better AI experiences.

Strategy 3: Automate RAPTOR – Structured Prompting

If you're building automations or prompt chains using tools like:

- Zapier or Make (for workflows)
- LangChain, LlamaIndex, or OpenAI API (for developers)
- Custom SaaS tools with embedded LLMs

you can design prompts using RAPTOR sections as modular inputs.

Example: Automation Workflow

- A user submits a service incident summary
- A script auto–fills RAPTOR fields:
  - Role: Incident response analyst
  - Aim: Summarise the event for the service review board
  - Parameters: Include timeline and impact; exclude internal IPs
  - Tone: Formal, passive
  - Output: Markdown–formatted report
- The LLM processes this and posts the result to the correct channel or ticket

RAPTOR becomes an API–driven logic model, enhancing quality at scale.

Strategy 4: Use RAPTOR for Prompt Governance

As prompting becomes embedded in more business processes, governance matters.

Use RAPTOR to:

- Create prompt approval workflows
- Ensure AI outputs adhere to tone, compliance, or branding guidelines
- Audit how AI is used across departments
- Train reviewers to assess prompts using the RAPTOR checklist

Just as code reviews improved software development, prompt reviews improve AI development.

Strategy 5: Foster a Prompting Culture

Beyond tools and templates, the most scalable way to expand RAPTOR is through **culture**.

Encourage:

- Regular prompt share–outs during team standups or retrospectives
- Cross–functional collaboration on prompt design
- Prompt libraries with version control or contribution credits
- Reward systems for improving prompts that power key workflows

Treat prompt design as a craft – not just a technical input, but a skill worth developing and celebrating.

Summary: Scaling RAPTOR in Practice

Approach	**Benefit**
Prompt Libraries	Reuse and refine high–performing prompts
Tool Integration	Guide non–experts to structured prompt creation
Automation with RAPTOR Inputs	Standardise quality in workflows and APIs
Prompt Governance	Align prompts with policies, compliance, and brand
Prompting Culture	Develop prompt literacy across teams

RAPTOR isn't just for writing prompts – it's a framework for scaling AI use responsibly and effectively across an organisation.

In our next and final section, we'll bring everything together – looking at how RAPTOR prepares you not just to write better prompts, but to become a prompt strategist in the age of AI.

The RAPTOR Mindset

RAPTOR is more than a framework – it's a way of thinking.

What began as six practical elements for designing better AI prompts has become something greater: a mindset rooted in intentionality, clarity, and collaboration with artificial intelligence.

In this final section, we'll reflect on what the RAPTOR framework truly enables – and how adopting the RAPTOR mindset prepares you to lead in the age of intelligent systems.

From Prompting to Thinking in Systems

At first glance, prompting seems simple – just type something and get a result.

But as you've seen throughout this book, effective prompting is not just about commands. It's about **communication**. It's about translating human goals into machine–understandable language, with precision and purpose.

RAPTOR teaches you to think in systems:

- To define intent before requesting output
- To guide AI with context, tone, and constraints
- To build feedback loops and allow for iteration
- To separate structure from style and strategy from syntax

That mindset will serve you across every tool, model, and platform – because it's not tied to any one technology. It's tied to how you think.

RAPTOR as an AI Literacy Tool

In a future where language models become embedded in everything – from writing assistants to workflow automations to decision–support tools – prompting becomes a form of **literacy**.

RAPTOR empowers you to:

- Communicate clearly with AI
- Design high–impact workflows
- Collaborate across technical and non–technical domains
- Lead conversations around risk, tone, and audience
- Uplift others by teaching them a structured, confidence–building method

This makes you not just an AI user – but a **translator**, an **enabler**, and a **strategist**.

RAPTOR in Your Toolkit

Here's what the RAPTOR mindset looks like in practice:

When you	**You're using RAPTOR thinking**
Ask who the AI should be before giving it a task	**Role**
Focus on one core goal per prompt	**Aim**
Define scope, references, and constraints	**Parameters**
Align the communication style to the audience	**Tone**
Design the result with reuse and clarity in mind	**Output**
Treat prompts as prototypes and iterate with care	**Review**

This is not a rigid checklist – it's a dynamic habit of mind. You'll find yourself applying RAPTOR without thinking: during meetings, while drafting automation workflows, or even when helping others think more clearly about what they want from AI.

You Are Now a Prompt Strategist

By reaching this point, you've gone far beyond just knowing how to write prompts.

You've become something rarer: a **prompt strategist**. Someone who:

- Designs systems, not just single interactions
- Anticipates how AI can best support different roles and goals
- Builds prompts that respect context, tone, format, and compliance
- Coaches others to think with clarity, not just speed

- Understands that prompting is a skill – one that reflects real–world thinking

In the future, this capability will be foundational. Businesses, schools, and governments will need people who can bridge the gap between what we want and what AI understands.

That's you now.

What Comes Next

Your RAPTOR journey doesn't end here. In fact, it's only beginning.

Here are a few directions you can take next:

- Build a personal prompt library using RAPTOR–structured examples
- Create workshops or internal guides to teach others the framework
- Adapt RAPTOR to your specific field – legal, medical, creative, engineering
- Contribute back by evolving the framework, extending it, or sharing your own applications
- Stay curious – AI tools will evolve, but structured, intentional communication will always matter

And remember: a single good prompt can save hours. A well–designed prompt system can save organisations.

Final Words

You've learned how to think like a designer, communicate like a strategist, and collaborate like a leader in the age of AI.

You've equipped yourself – and others – with a toolset built on clarity, context, and care.

RAPTOR

The AI Prompt Engineering Framework

Now go forward.

Build with intent.

Lead with clarity.

Let your prompts rise on the wind of purpose, shaped by thought, guided by a newfound vision.

RAPTOR Tools

The tools on the following pages are designed to help you put the RAPTOR Prompt Engineering Framework into action. Use them as quick references, build them into your workflow, or share them with your team to promote consistency, clarity, and creativity when prompting AI systems.

1. RAPTOR Prompt Template and Checklist
A structured template to guide users through each of the six RAPTOR elements –**Role**, **Aim**, **Parameters**, **Tone**, **Output**, and **Review**. It's designed to help beginners build well–formed prompts from scratch and assist experienced users in maintaining consistency. The accompanying checklist ensures no element is overlooked and promotes disciplined prompt development.

2. RAPTOR Review Checklist
To be used during the final stage of the RAPTOR process, this tool helps assess the clarity, completeness, and impact of a prompt. It encourages reflective evaluation after testing, helping to identify what works, what doesn't, and how to iterate more effectively.

3. RAPTOR Meta Prompt Template (Cheatcode)
This is a self–referential prompt about prompting that allows users to generate RAPTOR–aligned prompts using AI itself. By requesting the model to fill in each RAPTOR element, this cheatcode can accelerate workflow, unblock creative hesitation, and serve as a training tool for teams.

1. RAPTOR Prompt Template and Checklist

A structured, fill-in-the-blanks template for designing high-quality prompts. Includes a step-by-step checklist that ensures each RAPTOR component (Role, Aim, Parameters, Tone, Output, Review) is clearly addressed before deploying a prompt in production.

Role: ______________________________

Aim: ______________________________

Parameters:

- ___________________________
- ___________________________
- ___________________________

Tone: ______________________________

Output: ______________________________

Review: ______________________________

2. RAPTOR Review Checklist

Use this tool to audit, improve, or refine existing prompts. It provides key questions to assess whether a prompt aligns with its original intent, avoids ambiguity, and produces useful and reusable outputs. Ideal for teams adopting prompt governance or quality control.

Element	?	**Comments**
Role		Is the AI's persona clearly defined?
Aim		Is the task focused, singular, and actionable?
Parameters		Are constraints, sources, and context provided?
Tone		Does the tone suit the audience and task?
Output		Is the structure, format, and medium defined?
Review		Does the prompt allow for reflection, iteration, or clarification?

3. RAPTOR Meta Prompt Template (Cheatcode)

A prompt to write prompts, this cheatcode lets AI help you generate a complete RAPTOR-aligned prompt by describing your goal or idea in plain English. Perfect for beginners or fast-paced prototyping sessions where clarity and structure are needed immediately.

Use the template below to generate a complete and production-ready AI prompt using the RAPTOR framework. It's ideal for guiding an AI to co-create meaningful output.

Instructions: Copy the following meta prompt into your favourite LLM chat, not forgetting to add in your idea or task at the bottom. You can then either copy and paste the output into a new chat or ask the LLM to continue:

> Help me generate a complete and production-ready AI prompt using the RAPTOR framework:
>
> - **Role** Define the AIs persona.
> - **Aim** Set a clear task.
> - **Parameters** Establish scope and constraints.
> - **Tone** Determine communication style.
> - **Output** Specify the response format.
> - **Review** Enable iteration or refinement.
>
> I'll describe my goal briefly–please expand it into a full RAPTOR prompt that will guide the AI to build the actual end product (e.g. a functional application, tool, or system).
>
> **My idea or task:** [INSERT YOUR IDEA HERE]

About the Author

Warren A. Stockdale is an information security and AI strategy practitioner with a background in cyber operations, prompt engineering, and systems thinking. He holds an MSc in Cyber Security from Lancaster University and a B.A (Hons) in Human Rights from the University of Central Lancashire.

He created the RAPTOR framework to empower individuals and teams to think clearly and communicate intentionally with AI.

This is his first published framework.

References & Further Reading

- OpenAI. (2023). Prompt Engineering Guide. *https://platform.openai.com/docs/guides/prompting*
- Anthropic. (2024). Claude Model Context Protocol (MCP). *https://www.anthropic.com/index/claude-context*
- Reynolds, L., & McDonell, K. (2021). Prompt Programming for Large Language Models: Beyond the Few-Shot Paradigm. *arXiv:2102.07350*
- Liu, P. et al. (2023). Pre-train Prompt-based Instructions: Language Models Are Better Few-shot Learners. *NeurIPS*
- Hinton, G. (2020). The Bitter Lesson. *https://www.cs.utexas.edu/ eunsol/courses/data/bitter_lesson.pdf*

License and Use

www.ingramcontent.com/pod-product-compliance
Lightning Source LLC
LaVergne TN
LVHW022118200926
848481LV00003B/1190
9781036919269